The Magic of Transformation

Igniting & Manifesting
Your Soul Desires

By Nadia S. Krauss

The Magic of Transformation:

Igniting & Manifesting Your Soul Desires

By Nadia S. Krauss

As You Wish Publishing, LLC
Connect@asyouwishpublishing.com

www.asyouwishpublishing.com

ISBN-13: 978-1-951131-18-0

Library of Congress Control Number: 2021906172

Printed in the United States of America.

Nothing in this book or any affiliations with this book is a substitute for medical or psychological help. If you are needing help please seek it.

Table of Contents

Who should read this book?

"In this overstimulated society we live in: stop managing your time and start managing your focus."
—The 5 am Club

We both know that our time, energy, money, and resources are precious in this lifetime, yet we often waste them. I, for one, am not here to waste any of it. So I am cutting right to the chase; let me be upfront and crystal clear on exactly who I wrote this 100-page, helpful short book for.

Beginning this welcome with clarity on my behalf that I am not here to waste your time, energy, money or resources, is a laser-focused way to help you untangle from overstimulation as well as sacrificing your resources instead of building them.

This book is for the person who is NOT concerned about:

- Adding to the already large amount of noise existing in the world.
- Following trends just because everyone is.
- Promoting busy and complex for the sake of looking successful.

- Spending hours and hours of your life with things that, in the end, do not matter.

This book IS for the person who is focused on:

- Intuition and clarity creating the magic of your transformation and conscious manifestation.
- Re-connecting to your inherent power, heart, and soul.
- Finding answers through your inner guidance system.
- Being in-tuition to take aligned action.

Now let's identify who exactly I wrote this book for:

You, my friend, first and foremost value uniqueness, originality, and open-mindedness. You excel in the creative areas of your life and run your career, business, and life motivated by freedom, individuality, exploration, and self-expression. Your clients and the people you work with feel your passion and zest for life and often tell you how inspired and intrigued they are by you.

Fiercely independent, you march to the beat of your own drum. You transform and innovate, catalyze ideas, change, and manifest your visions. Often a pioneer in your field, you have found your purpose as a dynamic and intuitive entrepreneur in the world of business ownership. Freedom of expression is at the core of your identity. You always try to do work you have a real passion for, and following your bliss and joy has never steered you wrong.

But to all of this brilliance, there also comes a downside, a shadow that can cast its darkness over you. Never lacking ideas and never short on energy, riding the wave of enthusiasm, you can tend to take on too many responsibilities all at once. Which easily has you feeling unproductive because you find yourself frozen in overwhelm. You feel like you just don't have enough time to do all the things you want to do. Independent by nature, you might avoid anything that, in your perspective, impedes your freedom. Sometimes you even feel confined in a one-to-one relationship.

Being unattached to the outcome of your ideas or not finishing things you started has led you to identify with the starving artist and scattered dreamer syndrome, at times. And although you have overcome many obstacles in life and business, for the most part, not committing to a very specific thing can lead to you not being able to profit from the benefits that can come from specializing.

Make no mistake. I am not going to try to change your style or tell you what to do. Instead, this book is going to offer you companionship when the shadow of your brilliant self casts its spell. We are going to engage in stimulating conversation and laughter. We are going to appreciate each other's grand visions and the great stories we have to tell. Affectionately I accept the brilliant dreamer in you and the forever seeker of beautiful and unique self-expression.

This book ultimately is about having the guts to take risks by questioning the current status quo and believing that something even better is possible.

My Promise to You

If you are still with me, I promise not to waste the next hour or so of your life. Instead, I am going to show you how you can further utilize the magic of transformation: clarity + intuition = conscious manifestation. I am going to teach you how to go even deeper in your unique self-expression to excavate your gifts and Divine self. It is my greatest hope that this short little book will be a helpful new option for you to do what you do best while also addressing the shadow aspects of your brilliance.

Anybody who knows me knows that I tend to be radically honest rather than fake, straight to the point and heart of the matter, I like to go deep, and I detest wasting energy with unnecessary noise and complexity.

I promise to do my part and give you a tried and tested formula for igniting your Soul desires, harnessing your Soul fire to make all your dreams come true, and affectively applying Soul medicine to address those areas that are blocking and restricting you in your glorious expansion, growth, and next-level self. In return, I need you to do your part too. Commit to read this book in its entirety and with an open mind and heart.

It is my sincerest hope that what I am about to share with you will be:

- The most helpful way to connect to your power, heart, and Soul.
- The smartest formula for organic, natural growth and expansion into your greatest life.
- The fastest way out of entanglement and mis-alignment and back to your best self.
- The easiest path to Divine self-expression and a fully embodied brilliant life.

Of course, if you want or need more details than what I can include in this short, little book, you can check out my work by visiting my website (www.happywholesomelife.com) or befriending me on Facebook (Nadia Shana Krauss).

Introduction

There are two things I want you to know about me right from the start. The first is that as of the day that I am writing this, my experience with the Magic of Transformation and igniting Soul desire, harnessing Soul fire, and applying your Soul medicine, is 31 years and counting. The second thing is that I graduated from Medi-Wellness College in Cologne, Germany, with a degree in holistic health and wellness coaching, which is all about addressing the mind-body-spirit connection.

This is the first book I am publishing, in a series of books that will be published to address holistic understanding and insight in life that includes the Soul's perspective. Holistic means that you understand the importance of the whole while also having insight into the interconnectedness of its parts.

My track record of walking my talk and taking my own medicine is long and successful. Ask any of my friends, family, current, and past clients. I lead by example. Everything I share in this book is true, tried, and tested through personal experience and teaching the Magic of Transformation to my clients so that they may ignite their Soul desires while harnessing their Soul fire, also known as vital life force energy, in alignment with their dreams and truest self (Soul). The more I am helping my clients with this, the more I realize five important realities:

1. Society and parenting have shaped us into who we are, and rarely do we know or understand who we are at the Soul level.
2. There often is a huge gap between the connection of Soul with personality in this lifetime.
3. Working against the grain of your heart and Soul and favoring your Ego's personality or cultural conditioning slowly but surely depletes and disconnects us from our vital life force energy. It then becomes harder and harder to feel energized, happy, and healthy.
4. The more disconnected we are from our true heart and Soul, the harder it gets to experience our birthright of abundance to create wealth in our lives.
5. At this point, my clients usually find me, and together we apply the method and modality of Soul Realignment so that my clients can reclaim their power, sovereignty, and fully flowing life force energy in this lifetime.

My clients, and the women who are attracted to my work, are not content with the norm or the accepted status quo, and they are prepared to take great risks in moving themselves forward and closer to what they know they truly require, desire, and deserve. They view growth and personal development as an exciting adventure that will expand them into their next greater self. Their next-level vision is the perfect type of motivation that makes it so easy, graceful, and fun for me to work with them. I help them solve their problems from the five realities above I just shared.

Your next level requires:

- internal motivation,
- that represents an organic and natural way to grow,
- while also integrating all your desires, requirements, and needs in life.
- a re-inventive way, customized to your uniqueness.
- Soul Realignment and applying the Soul medicine that will instigate the great change, the big shift, and the magic of your transformation.

If you have ever wanted to find an organic and natural way to change that also feels like a deeply nourishing flow, then this little book is your passport to success!

Please note, I am going to spend zero time trying to convince you that the Magic of Transformation is real and that the power of Soul Alignment ignites your desires to come true by providing you with great amounts of life force energy to make them happen. While simultaneously also providing the medicine that integrates all of you into your wholeness. My assumption here is that you want to honor your uniqueness, your freedom, and your self-expression on a Soul level. You truly want to live your Divinity on this earth and be part of the solution this world so desperately needs. You want to fulfill your social promise and are totally up for creating your little piece of heaven here on earth in the process.

Get comfortable, brew yourself a cup of tea, grab your journal and a pen, and get ready for an illuminating journey that will lead you to Soul Realignment and the magic of your transformation.

If you have any questions or comments, feel free to reach out to me at

Nadia@happywholesomelife.com, and if you want to discuss working with me, schedule a Soul Realignment Blueprint Session with me at

https://happywholesomelife.as.me.

Enjoy the journey and the magic,

Nadia

P.S. When you're done reading, would you please leave an honest book review on Amazon? Reviews are the best way to help others, and I check all my reviews looking for helpful feedback.

Chapter 1
Igniting Soul Desires

"Don't judge each day by the harvest you reap but by the seeds that you plant."

—Robert Louis Stevenson

Planting the Seed

I want to start by stating that I have no problem whatsoever with 'living in the real world.' However, in today's world, there is a palpable disconnect between mind, body, and spirit and because of this disconnect, marketing and sales thrive on honing into immediately satisfying the ego with its desire for instant gratification. No major marketing campaign of any renowned company talks of seeding, watering, tending, fertilizing, cultivating, and growing, as the process to harvest all your wildest dreams and desires, no. Instead, it is suggested that success is immediate and takes no effort whatsoever.

At the end of the day, the Ego's desire for instant gratification is very inefficient, ineffective, and ultimately not very smart. Following your Ego desires costs you a lot of time, energy, and money. Nature's way is much smarter, more abundant, more effective, and efficient in regards to longevity. So this chapter is all about planting seeds to ignite your Soul's desires.

Just like Ego desires bear the quality of instant gratification, Soul desires carry the quality of expansion and growth. Soul desires are truly about growing yourself into the next level expanded version of yourself. Planting these kinds of seeds will have you fall in love with the journey of being the best version of yourself while also honoring your true nature.

What plants a seed of Soul desire?

Inspiration

Empowerment

Upliftment

Joy

Intuition

Passion

Enthusiasm

Optimism

Positive expectation

Alignment

Belief in your inherent power and sovereignty.

Utilizing your power.

Taking Soul-aligned action.

Making conscious choices based on your power, heart, and Soul.

Voicing secret dreams.

Owning hidden desires.

Growing yourself into your next level version through nourishment, nurturing, and support.

Cultivating the Magic of Transformation.

Applying the Soul Realignment modality.

Rather Than Fueling Your Ego Desires, Begin Planting Soul Seeds In Your Life

Let me demonstrate with a short story of how my dad planted the seeds of Soul in my life between the ages of 12 and 14, coupled with beautiful Divine synchronicity taking place.

I remember clearly the early days of adolescence. Being 11 years old, 12, 13, 14. I remember being talked to a lot by my dad, who was in the process of rediscovering his spirituality and connection to the Soul. He had read many self-help and new age books and at the time often held monologues to me about the things he was learning about. I liked listening to him because what he was saying inspired and intrigued me, and my young mind was soaking up all this knowledge he was sharing and the wisdom he had found in books. My mum was also reading the books but worked through them more as an introvert.

I remember dad and mum each in their way urging me on to live the best life that I possibly could. They believed that a better life was always attainable. They instilled my younger self with hope, optimism, positive expectancy, and belief. Their openness to life and their positive disposition encouraged me to believe in my highest dreams from a very young age and my capacity to also be able to manifest them in my life.

But as it would, life had a flip side to it. I also remember them struggling through life as the years went by. Stuck in the same story and stories over and over again. No matter what they tried, it always came back to two things in their life: relationship drama and money drama. It was a story of karma that had been created on a Soul level lifetimes before this life they were in now. But they did not know that at the time, neither were they provided the tools they needed to course-correct this situation. They did, however, put their daughter on the path of finding out. Discovering the tool of Soul Realignment and karma clearing along the way.

Dad always told me: "Nadia, you can have anything you want in life; you just have to discipline your mind to think the right things." While Dad had one part of the equation right, he was also still missing the bigger, holistic picture view, my adult self now realizes.

Mum always told me: "Nadia, no matter who you marry, make sure that you can communicate with your partner.

Communication is everything in a marriage. Without it, it is not a partnership based on love and respect. And there won't be a willingness to change when change is due." Mum didn't say or talk as much as my dad, but when she did, she always made a very clear point.

These talks my parents had with my younger self shaped me and my life experiences. Both mum and dad most definitely ignited Soul desire within me and planted plenty of seeds. It has been my desire to grow those seeds ever since and my firm belief that growing those seeds would expand me into my next level absolute self.

REFLECTION AND INTEGRATION

- What seeds were planted in your childhood?
- Have those seeds flourished or withered?
- What new seeds could you plant today that serve your expansion, growth, and next level?
- How can you nourish the relationship with your Soul desires?
- How do you nourish your heart?
- What can you do today to encourage your growth and potential?

Chapter 2
Discovering Utopia

The seeds that mum and dad had planted in my young mind found their fertile soil when my teenage self discovered a book that was just perfect for me. Deeply touching and magical, it announced what would become my life purpose.

It was bright blue. On the cover, a woman in a bathing suit, jumping across the beach. Immediately spellbound by the feeling of aliveness and vitality the book cover exuded, I cherished the energy the photo captured as she was at the highest point of one of her jumps. It made it look like she was flying.

The title of the book was mesmerizing to me as I read in large, white letters: *Ultra Health: The Positive Way to Vitality.* I remember opening that book in great anticipation of what I would find inside. My teenage self wanted to fulfill the promise that this book was revealing. With every page I read, I noticed a feeling expanding in my chest. My whole heart space exuded a state of absolute bliss as this new information revealed itself.

I was 14 years old at the time, in the middle of my puberty. In the phase of exiting childhood to enter adolescence as a young woman. I didn't feel particularly comfortable in my skin or body yet. The image on the book cover evoked these strong feelings – "Yes! That's what I want to look like! Yes! That's how I want to feel!"

My fire of fascination was lit, truly ablaze with passion for this topic! And with every new perspective the author unraveled for me in regards to health, wellness, and vitality, I felt this big, fat "YES!" expanding deep inside my heart. When she asked me if I could imagine jumping out of bed in the morning, full of energy, looking forward to my day, full of joyful anticipation, I heard this big, fat "YES!" within my chest. And when she asked me if I could believe in leading a life full of vigor and vitality, looking good and feeling fantastic as I age, and living my life with the same intensity and passion as in my younger years, I felt a clear, big, fat whole body "YES!" and "Heck yeah!" At that moment, my Soul fire was lit, and my Soul desire was discovered. I just knew: That's exactly how I wanted to live my life! There was no turning back now.

Today I realize that this book and this moment was a key experience in my life. Today I know that this "YES!" of mine that I felt so strongly and with great intensity manifested a very heartfelt intention that came from someplace deep in my Soul. Out of the depth of my being, my life would not have it any other way but to unfold in pursuit of health, wellness, and vitality. Experiencing a state of bliss and balance—physically, emotionally, mentally, and spiritually—not only became my vision but also my mission.

But what I didn't know, back then, was that at this royal moment in time, I gave my consent to go on a very bold, courageous, and adventurous journey. A journey on which I would experience the magic of my transformation to discover utopia or, more specifically, Soul Realignment.

A journey where 7 keystone areas in mind and heart set began shaping my life experience:

1. Did you ever wonder what it was like to feel great most of the time?
2. To awaken in the mornings looking forward to each day?
3. To enjoy the work you do, and to give it your all, to be blessed with plenty of energy to spare at the end of your days for pleasure and play?
4. To look terrific and to feel good about yourself and your life?
5. To know you have everything you need to meet whatever challenge you may face?
6. Sounds like a utopian dream?
7. It is not. It is something within your grasp!

Something Called the Magic of Your Transformation

My journey did not end with reading the last few pages of that book. The book did not contain all the answers I was seeking. There was still so much more information I needed to ultimately create this vision of my utopia and this mission of my life purpose.

Today, I am not only the dreamer but also the dream. 45 years of age, joyously entering into my wisdom years. I have learned so much in regards to “Ultra Health,” discovering utopia, Soul Realignment, and the Magic of Transformation.

I have also experienced the dis-ease that occurs when the mind-body-spirit connection in life is not understood, cherished, or upheld. In the last three decades, I got to know myself in a completely new way—through the magic of my transformation. I have matured from a child to an adolescent to a young woman. And from a searching, young woman to a calm, grounded, nourished, knowing woman anchored in her midlife wisdom.

Today this little book is my invitation to you. I reach out my hand to you with the intention to touch your heart. Sparking your heart’s wisdom by sharing my journey and nuggets of truth with you, I invite you to embark on the path of your magic and Soul dreams so you can find your unique way in utter and beautiful Soul alignment. My voyage has led me to a state of absolute joy and delight in my life. And my wish for you is the same.

Today I experience joie de vivre like the French like to say. It is an exuberant enjoyment of life anchored in vitality, peace of mind, contentment, gratitude, all-encompassing health, purpose, and meaning in my life. I truly wish this gift of living, connected to your heart and Soul as an embodied being of Divinity, on every woman I know, every man that I meet, and every person that has ever wondered it possible. It is my greatest hope that every child has the parents, guardians, and mentors it needs to remember their Magic of Transformation. If every human being were able to tap into this kind of power, our world's biggest problems would cease to exist because we would find the soul-utions to heal every single challenge we are facing as humanity today.

The path of heart and Soul isn't necessarily an easy one, but it is one of reverence, and it is sacred in its experience. Often there are big hurdles to overcome. Today I am reaching my hand out to you to make this process easier and less threatening in its vastness! I want you to know that you do not have to walk this pioneering path of courage, healing, uniqueness, and strength alone. I am your friend in this.

Remember…

"You Are The Dream & The Dreamer"

By Hal Price

There's a time and place for everything.

My heart tells me it's true.

There's a DREAM inside each living Soul,
An idea inspired by YOU!

There's a dream the world needs desperately,
It can touch brave hearts and minds.
It was seeded when you first were born,
It birthed you at the perfect time!

You're the gift the world has waited for!
You're the spark that lights the flame.
Your heart will feel this bright idea
When your big dream calls your name!

You were placed here for this special dream.
Life's great needs inspired each clue.
And you're humbled when you realize
That your magic dream…dreamed YOU!

REFLECTION AND INTEGRATION

- Does your dream make your heart skip a beat?
- Does it stir something deep within your being, your Soul?
- Does it express your passion for life in simplicity?
- Does it align with your core values and beliefs?
- Will it help you outgrow your comfort zone?
- Was it inspired by Divine guidance and intuition?
- Does your dream offer good and useful benefits for others?
- Does pursuing this dream support your growth and expansion?
- Does it feed your heart and mind?

Chapter 3
Mentors

As my mum and dad introduced me to personal growth and spiritual development, I recall books by Catherine Ponder speaking about the universal laws of prosperity, books by Joseph Murphy introducing the idea of positive thinking and improving your life, books by Norman Vincent Peale showing me that *You Can If You Think You Can*, and a certain book by John Kehoe called *Mind Power* giving me very specific instructions to manifest a dream.

Thinking back on this last book makes me smile because I recollect very clearly how I carefully applied its contents to my life, following suggested exercises, and showing up for all this book had to offer me. At the time, I was 18 years old and was dreaming of a boyfriend and the romantic dates we would go on. I followed the very specific instructions to manifest my new boyfriend. It was hard for me to visualize his face in the suggested visualization exercises because, of course, I would not know what he would end up looking like, so I gave him a name instead.

I named my imaginary boyfriend 'Eric.' And from here on out, I would visualize, almost daily, what going on wonderful dates with Eric would feel like. I would envision the places we'd go to and the fun we'd have there together.

Looking back on it now, I realize it was an experiment. I enjoyed the visualizations, and I had a youthful optimism that this might just work. There was a sense of adventure ahead, and I remember it feeling light, playful, and it was easy to keep showing up for this imaginary world because it was fun.

Now the next thing that I am going to share with you might seem strange to you, and you might want to write it off as a coincidence, but three months later, I met a boy at a club. Attracted to each other, we were inching closer and closer on the dancefloor. Dancing and grooving to tunes like "Whoop There It is" and Salt N'Peppa's "Push It." The year was 1994.

We danced before we even spoke, and when we did speak a little later at the bar, we introduced ourselves. I was awestruck when I heard him say: "Hi, I'm Eric." (I kid you not!)

Let me tell you one more thing, and again I am not kidding: Eric and I ended up dating for two years, after which we got married, and in April 2021, we are celebrating our 25th wedding anniversary. (I know, right?)

My parents introduced me to the world of books, personal growth, spiritual development, and how these books came alive for me as mentors when I implemented their insight and wisdom into my life. The seeds of possibility were planted at a very young age, and as a young adult, I was sent living proof that this stuff works.

Since the time I was 11 years old and given my very first self-help, personal development/growth and positive thinking book by my father, I have been hooked on being 'mentored' by books. I seemed to have an innate ability to tap into the essence of a book to magically receive its healing activation. Books came alive for me and felt like I had mentors and teachers guiding me through life. Books lived close to my heart and still do. That is why I am now writing this one.

Books have supplied me with soul medicine. They have ignited my soul desire over and over again so that I can find the motivation to live my soul purpose life, livelihood, and business. They have taught me to harness my soul fire to do good in the world and to fulfill my social promise. Now you might be thinking, "Come on, Nadia, really, books? If it only were that easy!" And you are right, there is more behind the story than I am letting on, right this minute, but I promise we will get to this little secret of mine I never knew I had. Just keep reading. You see, this very special relationship with books, I would only come to understand much later in my life. Two more decades later, to be exact. But for you, the reader, it's only a few chapters down the line. Now isn't that great?

My little secret revealed itself through the magic of my transformation and the book of life itself. But, as I said, more on that down the line. For now, I want you to use your imagination. Imagine you had a superpower: the superpower to tap into the essence of a book to magically receive its healing activation. And within that healing activation, your superpower would also reveal to you exactly the things you need to do next to get what you say you want.

I know that we as humans have a tendency to look for answers outside of ourselves, but I want you to know that part of the secret and its power to catalyze immense amounts of vital life force is to move in the right direction. And it comes from the ability to activate your 'inner teacher.' Let's look at the word intuition more closely: in – tuition. Who is the one teaching you to stay on a path true to you? Your inner teacher, of course!

Have the heart to start connecting to your inner teacher and in-tuition right now. Let's begin!

- IMAGINE the book that holds the answers you are seeking.
- IMAGINE your heart space as a golden palace and a door opening within your heart.
- IMAGINE a throne within your heart space that you are sitting on now.
- IMAGINE reading the book with all the answers sitting on your heart space throne.

Now VISUALIZE a situation in your life that is not going as you wish it would have or had imagined, and then ask these questions:

1. WHAT exactly is happening in this situation right now? (Imagine seeing it from a higher vantage point.)
2. WHY is it happening exactly? (From this higher vantage point, are you able to detect patterns and occurrences that do not serve you or cause you pain?)
3. HOW can you change and transform this?

Let your inner teacher tell you more about the one baby step you could take to step outside of the pattern or occurrence that no longer serves you. Decide to follow your intuition. And then back up that decision with an action making it a powerful choice. Lather, rinse, repeat this process as often as you need to.

Next, I want you to write down the 4 aligned steps that your current situation visualization presented you with. They can be baby steps. Baby steps are really good in helping you grow outside of your comfort zone very naturally and organically. Then imagine that 4 baby step process helping you further expand and grow into abundance, success, peace, love, meaning, ‘ultra health,’ Soul purpose, and a positive way to vitality and joy. Ultimately helping you to create a happy, wholesome, abundant life from the heart. Step by step.

Take the time to do this now. Write it down.

Step 1:

Step 2:

Step 3:

Step 4:

Sit with the visualization and exercise, take the time to connect with your heart, your heart throne, and heartfelt questions regarding your current life situation. Just be in the moment, as is. Asking those 3 questions from a heartfelt space and truly wanting to know will instruct you about the possible next steps. Have a willingness to take action on these. Your action-taking will make them powerful choices that shape your life in a new and positive way.

Whenever something isn't going the way I had hoped or imagined, I make myself stop for a minute and connect to my breath and the presence of it in my body. This slows me down. And slowing down, I notice that I link with my inner guidance system, my inner teacher. When I slow down I can feel my heart, where my inner guidance and teacher live. And then in-tuition guides me. After I have received guidance, I can follow my higher purpose in life. I have found that following your higher purpose in life takes Soul Realignment.

Joined in this process of stopping, breathing, and slowing down, I begin to listen better. I listen better to all parts of me and stop seeking answers outside of myself and instead allow answers to arise from my heart and Soul, where my true power lies. That is truly the purpose of this exercise. Don't skip over it! Do it now. Set a timer for 5 minutes and do it. A decision to want to change is not enough. A decision made needs to be followed up with action. Then it becomes a choice. Make today's decision a choice by taking action. This does not have to be perfect. There is no right or wrong here. Just begin the journey of your magic and transformation by taking action. Take that first step that bears the potential to change your life for the better.

Making one choice at a time, from moment to moment, does not take long. Being beautifully aligned in the moment is powerful, I promise. Be assured there is no need to push for an outcome through this exercise. Right now, just show up for it and do it. Show up for yourself in this way. It only takes a few minutes. Be curious.

Chapter 4
Life's Checklist

"Become the change you wish to see in the world."
—Mahatma Gandhi

Dad told me that I could have everything I want in life. And even though he never fully found his healing activation to witness the magic of transformation manifest his desires, he was the one who opened me up to possibility while also helping me develop a positive disposition towards life. He briefed me on the happenings of the world on a grander scale: a spiritual awakening that would occur collectively in the years to come.

Because books had become my mentors, as I mentioned in the last chapter, it probably does not come as a surprise to you that I found exactly the book quadrilogy that would further explain what my dad was talking about. At the age of 24, I was reading *The Celestine Prophecy* by James Redfield. Through my heartfelt questions and continuously spending time on my heart throne, listening to my intuition, I started believing with every fiber of my being that there indeed would be a spiritual awareness in people that would lead to a spiritual and global awakening of sorts. An awakening to our Divinity that would make it possible for us, as the human race, to create heaven on earth. The possibility of discovering a utopia like this was a reality for me.

I recall that this deep innate knowing inside of myself was nourished, nurtured, and supported by a very firm decision I had made at age 11. That decision was prompted by yet another story Dad told me, followed by a question: "Nadia, imagine there was a world full of order, peace, abundance, love, compassion, kindness, freedom, collaboration, and prosperity for all. Working together for the highest good of all involved. And then imagine that there was a world full of chaos, war, fighting, power struggles, manipulation, strife, scarcity, and ego trips, where only a select few highly benefited from a system of oppression. Which world would you want to live in?"

Thinking back to it now, my younger self was surprised that he would even have to ask me that. I chose the latter. Dad helped me realize that my decision would need to be backed up by action because my younger self could also see that the other world he mentioned existed too. With Dad's help, I was able to discern which part of the world I wanted to have an impact on. I chose to be part of a new world order and a new era of spiritual awareness and awakening very early on in my life through my actions. And just like Gandhi said so wisely: I became, and am still becoming, the change I wish to see in the world through the magic of my transformation. Today I trust that I can be the spark for you to ignite that same Soul desire.

It is time we rise in the belief that we can discover utopia as the human race. Creating the experience of heaven on earth, manifesting collective dreams of Divine order, harmony, supportive structures of peace, abundance, love, compassion, kindness, freedom, collaboration, and prosperity for all. It is time we fully stand in our power and sovereignty to live out our humanity while also expressing our Divinity. So that our life's legacy may serve our greater good as well as that of all of humanity. And Mother Earth can heal and rejuvenate to provide a home with abundant nourishment for the next generations to come.

Diana Cooper's Vision Prayer, 2012

I have a vision where all people are at peace, fed, and housed.

Every child is loved and educated to develop their talents,

Where the heart is more important than the head, and wisdom is revered over riches.

In this world, justice, equality and fairness rule.

Nature is honored, so the waters flow pure and clear, and the air is fresh and clean.

Plants and trees are nurtured, and all animals are respected and treated with kindness.

Happiness and laughter prevail and humans walk hand in hand with angels.

Thank you for the love, understanding, wisdom, courage, and humility to do my part to spread the light.

May all the world ascend.

Dad helped me to plant the seed of my decision-making muscles and follow through. My heart watered my commitment to my dreams, and my mum supported the desires I had about myself and the world. My desires lit on a Soul level. I was always willing to boldly go where no one else had gone before, taking aligned action to manifest all I required, desired, and deserved. I know I earned great pride and admiration for that from my mum.

Decide. Commit. Succeed. Became my mantra. And this mantra asked of me my awareness, my consciousness, and my embodiment. Reflecting on this, I can see all the different stages of my life and what they have taught me. In a little while, I will provide you with that insight through 'Life's Checklist.'

But before I do, I want you to know that it was those long conversations that my dad had with me, and the spiritual seeking my parents went through, and the pain they experienced in their life, that has shaped me into the person that I am today. All of that sparked the need to ignite a deep desire within me. This deep desire ignited would serve me well as fuel and drive, urging me on throughout my life. It was that Soul desire ignited that gave me a sense of adventure. I was lit. Lit to take risks, to try something new by transforming the old into something bigger, better, and more whole-some. I was eager to get off the beaten path to forge my own. Utopia was always on the horizon for me.

"Go confidently in the direction of your dreams. Live the life you have imagined." —Thoreau

I found myself so eager, so enthusiastic, and so happy that I could be creating anything that I wanted. And that's how 'Life's Checklist' was born for me. Much like kids in America write a letter to Santa for Christmas, I wrote a letter to the Universe about my life and what I wished for. It was an immensely powerful feeling for me to realize that life offers us a lot of opportunities to do interesting and exciting things. Being young, I had the world at my feet. So I kept asking myself: "What is it that I would like to have and experience?" And deciphering and discerning that was easy because I just knew that I wanted it all. I wanted the good looks, the strong body radiating vitality, the zest for life, the soul mate relationship, the romance, the life purpose, and to be on a mission to make an impact, the money, prosperity and wealth, the health and longevity, the like-minded friends and community, the traveling, exploring, and adventure, but also taking time outs and retreating. I wanted it all and believed I could have it all. I still do.

Little did I know at the time that what I wanted to have and to create in my life would become the journey of what my Soul truly desired for me. My Soul desires unraveled what I would require, desire, and frankly deserve in my life. This grand adventure of getting everything I wanted was a journey back to self and connecting to my intuition and inner teacher through my heart's palace.

"You can have it all. Just not all at once." —Oprah Winfrey

The magic of transformation leads me back to my true nature and my Soul's calling. Up until the age of 28, I manifested the things I wanted with much gusto in life, and it usually didn't take too long for opportunities and exciting things to materialize in my world. But after the age of 28, I started noticing that there was a pattern I did not much care for: the big disconnect.

The Big Disconnect

I lost weight, exercised, and made over my body with an entirely new wardrobe and still found myself bullying my body, never happy with her.

I chased my ideal career, trying on one shoe after the other for fit, but it still completely eluded me for years.

I always followed my heart, my joy, my passion and was often thought of as the scattered dreamer and 'starving' artist by friends, family, and colleagues.

Getting an education in a specialized field did not seem as easy as I thought it would have been because my father did not plan for it and could not financially support me in this endeavor.

Making money seemed so hard and wasn't any fun at all. The whole topic of money was just so uncomfortable for me.

I did find my soul mate and got married young, which turned out to be quite the challenge as we tried to navigate through life together, barely knowing who we "were" ourselves. There were a lot of power struggles, and there was a lot of heartache for the first 10 years of our marriage before we could settle into being comfortable as individuals and as a couple.

We are Our Mothers and Fathers

Even though my parents did the best they could by planting seeds of grand visions in my young mind, they also could only work with what they had. We often face hurtful patterns that don't serve us and parents that instilled them in us because their parents instilled it in them before us. Parents, just like any other people, only know what they know. And when they know better, they do better. 'Positive thinking' alone isn't enough. It does not help us know better. Sometimes knowing better takes facing the reality of failure in life and tackling our inner demons head-on. And not everyone is willing or able to bravely face their failures. But when we do, we are gifted with detecting the patterns that no longer serve us. Detecting and transforming those patterns not only serves as healing for us but also as healing for our ancestral line. In the personal development world and spiritual growth community, healing those patterns is often referred to as healing the mother and father wound.

"Don't leave behind a legacy of self-abandonment." —Joy Balma

In the last 13 years leading up to finally writing this book, I have lived the life of transmuting and transcending these wounds. This now enables me to transform the pain my parents experienced. Because even though they were, generally speaking, positive people, there was a lot of pain in their lives. This helped me see and learn that the human experience often is the reality of a heavy leaden one. 'Positive thinking' alone does not transform this experience into light-filled spiritual gold. If it did, mum and dad would have aced that task.

I checked off many things on my want list, reached many goals for myself, but for years it seemed that every time I reached a goal, I realized that this thing I wanted didn't feel at all how I thought it would feel. Instead of feeling fulfilled, happy, and blissful, I felt empty, unhappy, and distraught.

In my enthusiasm and eagerness to find my life purpose, I found that being of service wasn't as appreciated by others as much as I thought it would be. Being of service to fulfill a mission that would make an impact, I felt more like a doormat than a powerful changemaker. For many years I had to learn that givers need to set boundaries because takers simply won't. It was hard to find time for myself and the very necessary self-care when there was just so much to do and reach on my 'Life's Checklist.' Taking care of myself well seemed like an impossible task for a very long time. And did not become a priority until my body caved in. I had to lose my health twice; stop, breathe, slow down, and start listening to my inner teacher: my intuition.

My 'life's checklist' started turning into a vision quest:

- Who am I?
- What am I all about?
- What is my true nature?
- How can I find balance, nurturing, happiness, nourishment, joy, and a wholesome approach to life that would sustain me?
- So that I may flourish, prosper, and thrive into the person I am truly meant to be?

I was not going to be able to positively think myself out of this emptiness, unhappiness, and distraught feeling at the pit of my stomach. I had to learn to know better, and sometimes knowing better takes facing the reality of failure in life and tackling your inner demons head-on.

'Life's checklist' turned 'vision quest' turned 'slaying inner demons.'

1. Overcoming body hatred and self-bullying.
2. Overcoming dis-ease.

3. Overcoming burnout and feeling numb inside.
4. Finding my ideal career pathway, and knowing exactly what it is and how to get it.
5. Learning how to discern between ego trips and Soul desires.
6. Knowing how to decipher what my Heart, Soul, and intuition are telling me so I can follow that calling.
7. Overcoming bankruptcy and healing my money relationship.
8. Learning to make friends with money.
9. Overcoming co-dependency and enmeshment.
10. Learning to be of service without self-sacrifice or self-abandonment.
11. Finding time for myself, sacred self-care, and retreat regularly.
12. Finding true Soul Realignment through the book of life itself.

Life's checklist was now null and void. It no longer mattered what I had achieved in the past because I was faced with looking at the mess that I had created in my life. All that mattered now was that I had reached ground zero. I had hit rock bottom. I was on a road of broken dreams, and I needed to know why. I couldn't believe what was happening. I had lost my way and was living in a world of doubt and feeling like a failure. I did not want to live this way. It was haunting me. I just needed to get it straight. Needed to stop wasting time. I knew I was living in a lie. It was time to choose a truer path. Life was supposed to be amazing, I thought. Why wasn't it amazing? That heartfelt question, asked in the space of my heart palace, forced me to look at my life with further questions, such as:

- Why was Utopia and Ultra Health eluding me?
- What happened to my little piece of heaven here on earth?
- And how did I end up manifesting my hell and disease instead?

I and my life felt broken. Feeling broken like this pushed me closer to the edge of my feelings, which helped me surrender my ego. I handed it all over to the Divine in a complete release. I asked Source to put me back together, to mend my broken pieces. I had so many unanswered questions. I could not grasp how I had gotten myself into such a dysfunctional mess. Facing my failure and inner demons, my mess transcended and transmuted into the message you are now reading in this book: Ignite your Soul desires. Apply Soul medicine. Manifest your Soul dreams. Harness your Soul fire. Witness the Magic of Transformation.

REFLECTION AND INTEGRATION

- What part of the storytelling in this chapter can you relate to?
- What stirs in your heart?
- What fog lifts from your mind reading this?

- What desires do you feel shook up in yourself?
- Are you currently finding yourself on a vision quest as well, to find more purpose and healing?
- Where does the pain lie in your life?
- Are you finding yourself overcommitted, over-whelmed, and entangled in a lie because you are desperately trying to prove your worth and that you are enough?

Chapter 5
When True Love Was About To Die

"Let the beauty of what you love be what you do."
— Rumi

"True Love is just the act of saying 'I choose you' every day." — Unknown

I recall it as clearly as if it were yesterday, and thinking about it, I can still feel the pain that was upon us on that Christmas morning. It was the Christmas of 2010. The one where we got into the biggest fight we had ever been in. It was huge because it was cold, destructive, and loveless. Never had that happened to us before. Never before did we simultaneously experience how love had left our hearts.

That day, as we were throwing accusations at each other, blaming the other for the situation and its unhappiness, this was the moment we realized that we had hit rock bottom as individuals and as a married couple. We were both so unhappy with our lives, our jobs, our money, our marriage. Ultimately that morning, we noticed that we were falling out of love. I was falling out of love with the man I had loved fiercely for 14 years. Never had I been faced with such a harsh reality ever before. The reality that we were both listening to the voice of ego and fear over the voice of love and true heart.

I still remember very clearly my husband speaking these words softly after all the terrible accusations had settled: "Or we could just choose to listen to love. We can choose to just follow love." His words stunned me. I wasn't expecting them. Surprised at how wonderful, beautiful, lovely, wise, and full of love this man was after all, I could feel my whole body relax.

Ultimately that was the day, the moment in time when we both chose to not let the love die and to find happiness together once again. Even though we were pretty miserable in that moment.

Looking back on it now, I know that we knew that we could not continue like this. We could not continue blaming each other for our unhappiness. We knew that we needed to find out what it was that would make us happy as individuals. But also as a married couple. And then we would need to tell each other what it was. The day we decided not to let the love die, we went on that journey together. The journey of finding love again and through it our happiness.

Together is a great place to be. Happiness is making a choice.

1. A choice to let go.
2. A choice to forgive.
3. Happiness is freedom.
4. Freedom to heal.
5. Freedom to connect.
6. Freedom to love yourself and each other.

Our hearts, Souls, and higher selves were calling us into purpose, to create our personal legends. The lessons we had to learn, the realities we had to transmute, transcend, and transform, stretched us to our absolute maximum. Because of our pain points in life, we were no longer able to ignore that love would leave the table if we'd allow it. We weren't willing to do that.

That fight and everything leading up to it was the transformational catalyst needed to make a radical, very much needed, life-altering decision. When our love was about to die, we made a drastic change.

It was 11-11-11 when we left Germany with only two suitcases and a backpack each to go live and work on a cruise ship. This extremely necessary act would not only save our marriage but also my broken life. It was on the ship that I began to understand the lessons of my life. I began to understand how I had created a living hell for myself instead of creating my little piece of heaven here on earth. I was no longer able to run or hide from myself. I had to look at my codependency, my chronic over-giving, self-sacrificing, and self-abandoning ways. I had to realize that in all my entrepreneurial endeavors, I struggled with setting boundaries and voicing my needs. I seemed to be constantly confused and fused to other people's needs and feelings but rarely aware of my own. I had become so disconnected from my intuition, desires, happiness, and self-care in my pursuit of proving my worth and enoughness that I didn't even know how to ask for support. Just when love was about to die, I woke up!

"Above all, choose to be the heroine of your life, not the victim." —Nora Ephron

I always had a dream of starting something on my own. I wanted to create things. As a teenager, I thought I would go on to study fashion design, but Soul made different plans for me. I never would have thought that I was going to be married at 20 years old.

After I met Eric at the 'Q' nightclub in Germany, I finished an apprenticeship in dressmaking to follow my interest in fashion design, but those plans changed after we got married because now I had a new commitment I wanted to uphold, our marriage. I did, however, stay true to starting something of my own.

I was 24 years old when I opened my very first business, a group training studio called "Fitness for Body & Soul." It was small, cozy, and all mine. I treated each of the members as if they were family and created a very intimate atmosphere that my customers loved. Even though I started something on my own and succeeded in creating it, I don't remember feeling victorious for very long. Instead, I remember trying to prove myself, my worth, and showing everybody that I was enough. I remember constantly chasing things. And these patterns of mine were very self-destructive and caused love to leave the table. I created several businesses that I loved intensely at the beginning and ended up hating immensely at the end.

This pattern went so far as to create and manifest a business relationship where my ex-business partner called me a loser because I chose love over entrepreneurship. She told me that my husband would be my downfall. I would never make it as a business owner because I just don't have what it takes. In her eyes, I was not a fighter. This happened before leaving Germany to go live and work on a cruise ship. Love had most definitely left the table in that business relationship. The event stuck with me for years, not only because those words really stung but also because part of me believed that about myself too. I did see myself as a failure. She was just rubbing salt in the wound.

The only thing that helped me through this pain of feeling like an utter failure was the undying love I carried in my heart for myself, my Soul, my Beloved, as well as the certainty that what she was saying about me and my life choices wasn't true. The strength of my spirit helped me see that she had meant to beat me while I was down because, leaving the business relationship, she felt hurt and betrayed. I had broken her trust. And while I got that, I also knew that relationships in life are here for a reason, a season, or a lifetime. We all have our life paths and life lessons. And mine was always based on where my heart and Soul were guiding me next. She was not able to understand that. There was no way I would have been able to explain this to her either. Even if I tried. Her perception of life, love, and business was very different than mine. My value system did not coincide with hers. So this relationship only lasted for a season and taught me to trust my heart, to stand in my power, to know my boundaries, and to communicate them fiercely.

It taught me that my heart knows best:

- How can choosing love over power struggles be wrong?
- How can choosing safety, steadiness, stability, and security to calm, soothe, and heal your nervous system be wrong?
- How can choosing passion, power, and potential over a draining situation be wrong?
- How can letting go of energy leakages that deplete time, money, and Soul focus be wrong?
- How can taking a time out to regroup be wrong?
- How can choosing divine guidance, ease, and grace over delusional ego plights be wrong?
- How can letting go of the fight, the hustle, the stress, the chasing after things madness, and the endless pursuit of feeling good enough and proving yourself be wrong?
- How can choosing what is right for me be wrong? Aren't those my choices to make in life and not yours?

In my heart and Soul, those choices could never be wrong because they help me stand strong in my power. And these choices and the actions I take when I fully stand in my power lead to growth, spiritual development, and expansion. In the end, that has always been what I wanted out of my life: growth, spiritual development, and expansion. My part in this little scenario of business and relationship drama was merely to choose how I would respond to the situation and those very hurtful and destructive words.

I chose to respond in self-love and in leadership true to myself. Through honoring myself with sacred self-care. Having my needs met to manifest all that I require, desire, and deserve. I knew I deserved better. Required more. And desired a whole different level of soul self-expression. I yearned for a business, a career, an income that reflected a livelihood that was connected to spirituality as its foundation. A livelihood that connected me to my Soul inherited abundance and balance. It took me on the journey of Soul Realignment to ignite the Magic of Transformation that creates your highest good.

Don't believe anyone about what it is that is supposed to make you happy and successful. Trust to know yourself and your needs. Forge your path. Listen to your heart and Soul to learn about what makes you truly happy. Know your value system and align with it. Define and build success on your terms in Soul alignment.

"Success is liking yourself, liking what you do, and liking how you do it." —Maya Angelou

At this point, I would like to remind you that if you need support in any of these areas—relationships, money, health, love, career, livelihood, prosperity, Soul purpose, and personal freedom—I am here for you. All you need to do is schedule a free Soul Realignment Blueprint Session with me by following this link:
https://happywholesomelife.as.me, and we can discuss how I might be able to support you.

Look back on your insights gained through answering the inquiry journaling questions of each chapter. In your answers, find how love is guiding you to do the right thing. If you currently find yourself at a crossroads in life, begin asking yourself the right questions while remembering to be in your heart, taking up space and taking your place on your heart throne.

Whenever you ask yourself these questions and hear the answer, you will feel a powerful realignment of your heart and Soul. You will feel the Love nourish your being.

1. Does it resonate with my heart & Soul?
2. Does it simplify my passion for life?
3. Does it align with my core values and beliefs?
4. Does it feed and nourish my heart and mind?

5. Will it grow me past my comfort zone?
6. Was it inspired by my inner guidance teacher and higher Self?
7. Does this path offer good and useful benefits for myself and others?

Chapter 6
From Mess to Message

"And the day came when the risk to remain tight in a bud was more painful than the risk it took to blossom."
—Anais Nin

2010 was the year that I had just built my third business successfully. Successful meaning that I was making money and serving clients. Successful meaning that I was attracting clients that wanted to pay me for what I offered, and I was generating money regularly. That's successful, right? Then how come everything felt like such a mess?

I was feeling completely drained and always lacking time and energy. The effort and time it took to generate the money felt overwhelming, incongruent, and in complete disharmony with what I wanted out of being a business owner. I could not understand why I had created yet another business and career path that I ended up hating. I could not understand that I created a business that just felt like another job once again. Where was my freedom hiding? Where had my independence gone? And where was that abundance I had hoped for?

I so desperately wanted to know what it felt like to have more than enough. More than enough time to do the things I love. More than enough energy to work and play equally. More than enough money to enjoy life. More than enough freedom. I wanted to know what it would feel like to be continuously presented with opportunities that would help me expand into abundance, love, success, health, and a business that felt soul-aligned. Soul aligned, meaning that my business utilized and self-expressed my god-given talents and gifts while I was being helpful, of service to others, and making a positive impact on this world.

From Not Feeling Enough to the Full Spectrum of Abundance

I so desperately wanted to know what it feels like to feel more than enough and to feel amply rewarded and cherished. I wanted to stop feeling like such a mess. I desired that kind of fulfillment. I wanted to stop being so rushed and driven in life without going or getting anywhere. And I wanted to stop creating things that I would end up hating.

How could I believe so fiercely that anything in life is possible, that I am a conscious manifestor of my life experience, and still end up creating a life and business that had me lacking and wasn't sustainable long term? A life and business that robbed me of my juice. My time. My energy. And my money. Daily. How could this have happened?

I was at a complete loss. I was. I wanted this hurtful reality of never feeling enough, no matter what I did, to be over. So I shut the doors to my self-employment in December of 2010 and got a job. I knew things had to change. But I did not know how. I also knew that my heart would always beat as a free-spirited creative, but until I had this figured out, I would just 'have to hang and wait it out.' Waiting it out turned into several years of life happening so I could learn and understand what my life was trying to teach me and how I ended up creating such a mess of it in the first place.

I had to make peace and come to terms with the fact that the patterns I was living had created the manifestation of lack and misalignment to the things that are truly important to me in life. Even though I had intended to build a business to create freedom, independence, and abundance for myself, my existing energetic patterns weren't serving that purpose at all.

The first step to turning my patterns around was boldly facing my current reality to look myself in the eye and ask: how can I overcome this self-defeating pattern of mine to adopt a new way of being in the world? One that serves me in creating freedom, independence, and the abundance I so desire?

1. I had to dive deep beyond surface-level solutions.
2. I had to get specific. I had to get clear on what it was that I truly wanted.

3. I had to become aware and mindful of vibrational misalignment in myself and my environment.
4. I had to surround myself with positivity, support, and encouragement.
5. I had to ditch the fear leaders and welcome in the cheerleaders instead.
6. And then to make some radical choices to boldly go where I had never gone before.

"Insanity is doing the same thing over and over again expecting different results." —Albert Einstein

It takes time to understand the mess so you can excavate the message. It takes time to shift yourself from not feeling enough into the full spectrum of abundance. It takes time to apply the Magic of Transformation to create the life you were born for. But if you are ready to move out of a reality that mirrors lack back at you and you desire to generate more abundance in every area of your life, then I am here today to tell you that it simply begins with a commitment to yourself. The commitment to love yourself through it, love yourself enough to do the hard things in life with follow-through.

In my experience, abundance was achieved the moment I realized that life is a direct result of how much a person chooses to love themselves as a Divine creation and their willingness to fully self-express the truest version of that creation. It often is also necessary to clear some old negative karma which we will get into in the next chapter.

Redefining Life, Love, Health, and Success

11.11.11 was the day hubby and I went on a vision quest together. That vision quest was dedicated to redefining our love, our life, our well-being, and our success. We were ready for ownership and self-determination to find answers to create the happy, wholesome, abundant life we were seeking as individuals and as a married couple.

Of course, our individual vision quests looked a little different, as do our desires, but as a couple in love, we do find common denominators, and many of my clients relate to these as well.

- We want to live a happy and peaceful life together, anchored in pristine simplicity, with more than enough money.
- We want to live in radiantly healthy and strong bodies to feel energized by life and living on purpose.
- We want to live in a fulfilled, harmonious, and balanced marriage, creating our personal legends together.
- We want to contribute to this life, to this world. We believe in winning big while doing good!

From Burnt Out to Filled Up From The Inside Out

"When the personality comes fully to serve the energy of its soul, that is authentic empowerment." —Gary Zukov

The answers to all of my questions were found in my journeying back to Soul Self. When I hit rock bottom, I had plummeted so deep and was so far off course that I had no choice but to get bold and real with myself.

I made a divinely and empowered choice:

- I chose to continuously and steadily show up for myself.
- I chose to live in the energy of nourishment, nurturing, and support of my Soul Self.
- I chose to hand over my desire for achievement, doership, and success to the heavens.
- Hitting rock bottom, I had no choice but to surrender to all of it.

It was very clear and obvious that 'my way' was not working. It was clear and obvious that it was time to try a new way! The time came to blossom, prosper, and flourish in a new way.

It took all of my courage, all of my inherent self-love, to boldly go places I had never gone. Discovering new territory I had never been on before. Beginning to be and do things in a very different way. It's a journey of personal growth, spiritual development, self-exploration, continuous discovery, insight, and mastery. My journey and walking the path allows me to share everything I have discovered about the Magic of Transformation with you, as well as revealing the Book of Life to you.

REFLECTION AND INTEGRATION

- How can you choose to continuously show up for your life?
- How can you choose to live in the energy of nourishment daily?
- Is your desire for doership, achievement, and success getting in the way of you hearing what heart and Soul are saying?
- What does surrender look like to you?

Chapter 7
The Book of Life

My parents got married late in life. My mum had me at 35 and had my brother at 41. As mentioned at the beginning of the book, my dad introduced me to spiritual growth and personal development concepts, as well as the idea that I am the creator of my life experience and reality. My mum introduced me to the concepts of mind power creating your desires. My parents both believed in the power of positive thought and the ability to manifest in co-creation with the universe. My parents also believed in karma and past lives. All of this knowledge was planted in my young mind as seeds of wisdom that matured in my consciousness over time.

Identifying the Divine Intent of my Lineage

My parents were spiritual seekers and warriors of the light who believed they could create the life they desired to also fulfill their social promise and purpose in this world. They wanted to win big and do good in the world. They never stopped dreaming of a better world for themselves and others.

Explore the Space Between Lifetimes

However, their marriage wasn't optimal, and their relationship was marked by a lot of hurt, pain, hardship, and karma they had with each other. Karma they brought in from another life to clear in this life. They did not know this consciously, and they did not have the tools at the time to clear any of it.

As a teenager, it became very apparent to me that my mum wasn't happy in her marriage, and my dad did not treat her with the respect, love, and admiration she truly deserved as a woman and mother. Although my mum wasn't happy in her marriage, she never found the strength to leave the man that caused her such misery until later in life. She was around 65 when she began her spiritual empowerment journey and, for over a decade, was on a mission to right the wrongs of her past. We shared many conversations about chakra healing, angelic celestial support, energy healing, clearing ancestral patterning that no longer serves us, letting go of energy dynamics that carried over from past lives so that we could do better in this one.

Identify and Clear the Unwanted Ancestral Influences on the Present

In chapter 3 of this book, I spoke to you about how books came alive for me as mentors and how I seemed to have an innate ability to tap into the essence of a book to magically receive its healing activation. What I didn't know back then is that I was accessing the archive of my Soul wisdom and its journey through the Akashic Records, also known as the Book of Life.

My intensely heartfelt questions, asked while sitting on my heart throne, acted like a pathway and a process to access my records through my heart chamber, with the help of my Soul and akashic team.

1. What is happening?
2. Why is this happening?
3. How can I change it?

When books started to come alive for me at age 14, I was given the higher vantage point or bird's eye view via the akashic masters, teachers, and loved ones. This I intuited at age 39. And the years following, I consciously began understanding that if my parents had the akashic tools of Soul Realignment, the insight to reading karma, while identifying blocks to love, they could have cleared and healed their relationship and all their money troubles, struggles, and strife in this life time.

This chapter is pulling together all the last chapters for you to help you understand how reading, clearing, and healing in the Akashic Records can help you realign to your Divinity and how in your Divinity you begin creating your life's purpose in alignment with your heart and Soul. In this sort of alignment, you become fully congruent in your being, and you begin manifesting big wins that not only serve you but also creates a massive win and social promise for the world. Soul Realignment can heal and clear old energetic patterns that have carried over from past lifetimes so that you can finally shift into the Magic of Transformation, igniting your truest Soul desires to manifest them in abundance within your Divine and Soul Self fully expressed life experience.

Healing Difficult Bonds or Ties

Let me summarize the storyline of this book so far so that you may see how you can find your narrative in mine. As you read the bullet points, find the points that have you self-identified and the ones that have you intrigued, wanting to find out more.

- Planting seeds of growth and expansion and the pain people experience even though they are masters of positive thinking and regularly practicing manifestation techniques in their life.
- Discovering utopia and the belief that we can all create what we want. It is possible to have it all in a natural progression and not all at the same time.
- How three intensely heartfelt questions had books come alive for me as mentors and how I opened up

my Akashic Records through this process but did not know it consciously at the time.

- How turning life's checklist into a vision quest helps you slay your inner demons. The demons that are holding you back.
- What to do when love is about to die and how to regain your true strength through love.
- How to go from feeling like a mess to embodying the messenger of your life values.
- Clearing old karma, healing old wounds, so you can begin creating your life anew in true Soul alignment, unlocking your Soul inherited birthright to abundance.

What are the Akashic Records?

"Think of the Akashic Records simply as an energetic database that stores every choice that we have ever made. The term Akashic Records is derived from the Sanskrit word "Akasha," meaning "ether." In Hindi, "Akash" means "sky" or "heaven." Rather than thinking of the Records as a single place, imagine them like an energetic information super-highway that resides outside of time and space." —Andrrea Hess

REFLECTION AND INTEGRATION

- Who are your ancestors?
- What are the distinguishing traits of your family tree?
- What might be the Divine intention of this line at soul-level purpose?
- How can you release the ancestral responsibilities that do not (and should not) belong to you?
- Do you have any guidance about how you can realize your soul-level intention/potential?
- And why you chose to reincarnate into this family group at this point in time?

Chapter 8
Mind-Body Medicine To Cure Disconnect

"Sometimes, the very soul medicine that you need to apply is the truth. Truth cuts through your BS and gives you much-needed clarity. Clarity creates speed and a path cleared from obstacles."

—Nadia Shana Krauss

Life is a journey. Life is an adventure. Life is a gift. And life isn't always easy. As you enter life in a spiritual context, you will notice that life is about what you decide it to be and what you are committed and devoted to. Life is about creating awareness around your conscious experience to embody and express your Divinity here on earth.

Applying your Soul's Medicine

1. You will have to let go of old programming that no longer serves your highest good. In this process of letting go, you will most likely encounter resistance, even self-sabotage, which then illuminates shadow aspects in your psyche and directs you to the wounds that need healing.

2. Sacred self-care is a critical factor for healing and for the Magic of Transformation to take place. You will be required to do it in your way authentically customized to your being. It will ask of you to trust your gut and to trust your Soul calling you to a purpose.

3. You will be encouraged to ask for Divine support and guidance. You are not in this alone. Your healing and transformation will accelerate exponentially when you choose to walk your Soul's path.

4. Your crystal clear, heartfelt and soulful WHY is necessary so that it can serve you as your North Star. Your heartfelt why supports you in staying connected to your truth.

5. Applying your Soul's medicine will require you to understand your money story. The narrative that keeps you stuck and blocked to receive more abundance in life so that you can do the thing you came here to do.

6. You might need to seek support to get past your old programming, resistance, self-sabotage, healing your wounds to rewrite the narrative that no longer serves you.

"Above all, choose to be the heroine of your life, not the victim." —Nora Ephron

While women pride themselves on taking care of their families and loved ones and their community contributions, they are also developing an awareness for their awakening. They are realizing that they cannot leave behind a legacy of self-neglect, as that serves no one. Sometimes letting the truth be told is exactly the soul medicine that you need, at a very particular moment in time. The moment in time when you are ready to hear it.

Women all over the world are beginning their Soul's healing journey to begin embodying the healed Divine Feminine in this world, as well as the Sacred Masculine in them. Most women in today's world feel a disconnect of some sort within themselves. Feeling disconnected is merely a symptom of what women require, desire, and deserve most:

- Connection to Self
- Connection to Body Wisdom
- Connection to Heart's Wishes & Desires
- Heart to Heart Connection with Others
- Connection to Higher Self
- Connection to Spirit Dream Team & Guides
- Connection to Source
- Connection to Soul's Purpose & Soul's Evolution

Women may not realize fully that the disconnect stems from them putting themselves last and putting everybody else and everything else first. Women today prioritize getting everything done for everybody else and put themselves last on the list. They often wear the cape of 'Superwoman' on their shoulders, never realizing that they are running themselves ragged.

They then often have to learn the hard way that running on empty serves no one. It just causes resentment and regrets in life. In their mind, they will tend to their personal needs, wishes, and desires once they have crossed off everything on their to-do list. But sadly, that means never getting to the parts of her day that are truly inspiring and empowering to HER.

As women, we are collectively awakening to another reality. One that is more natural and organic to the feminine way of doing things. It is a way of more balance between the awakened Divine Feminine and Sacred Masculine. Simultaneously we are also collectively waking up each morning and catapulting ourselves into the busyness of our days. We often carry very little regard for the many ways that we disconnect from ourselves in everyday life.

We keep reopening the wound of disconnect, never truly giving it the attention or the time that it needs to heal. Once we are willing to accept this truth, we also begin to understand that the experience of triumph and victory often eludes us, as the way we have chosen to live depletes us of our energy, time, and even money. Now let's talk about the 11 ways we potentially disconnect daily.

1. Being everywhere but here! Happiness always seems to lie in the future, in the next best thing, just around the corner. Let me ask you, where is your happiness NOW?

2. Our relationship to our body! Lack of self-love and acceptance. Lack of respect and forgiveness. Lack of connection to the Soul within your body.

3. No boundaries! Not knowing where we begin nor where we end. What our needs are and how to have them met.

4. Not having the necessary skillset! Not knowing how to nurture, nourish, and support ourselves and our well-being. Not knowing how to create physical health & happiness, mental calm, clarity & focus, emotional well-being & balance within a fast-paced lifestyle of demands and responsibilities.

5. Not understanding balance at the core! Missing the importance of natural rhythms and organic structure. Living life unbalanced within ourselves. There is a discord between the Divine Feminine energies and

the Sacred Masculine energies. One that we aren't even aware of.

6. Toxic living! A chronically stressful lifestyle. A complicated and complex life on all levels: physically, emotionally, mentally, and spiritually.

7. Trying to prove our worth! Deep down not feeling enough. Not feeling worthy. And not understanding nor knowing why this feeling is so deeply rooted.

8. Prioritizing things that truly have nothing to do with what we want! Chasing after egoic desires and accomplishments instead of connecting to heart and Soul's medicine so that all parts of us can become whole and integrated. The spiritual parts, the mental parts, the emotional parts, and the physical parts. Once we prioritize our higher path and align with Soul, happiness, healing, and wholeness do not lie far behind.

9. Not being mindful! Living outside of our bodies instead of in them! We live in a world of over-stimulating environments: Internet, Email, Facebook, Skype, Cell Phones. Ironically, in a world where we are constantly 'connected' on a physical level, we are depleting ourselves in ways of a spiritual connection.

10. Being way too hard on ourselves! Listening to the voice of fear versus the voice of love! Giving away too much room to the bully within as opposed to cultivating that strong, inner, kind, and nurturing voice.

11. Not knowing how to cultivate joy! Too many of us are not making time for the thing that most lights us up. Why does joy get put last? Because we are so disconnected from ourselves, we don't realize the value, the importance, and the sacredness of ourselves and how necessary joy truly is to our well-being.

Imagine Yourself Wired for Joy

Creating your world in affluence, joy, harmony, and peace. Creating your day playfully and luxuriously. Creating your life blessed and free, as you wish. Imagine yourself creating prosperity. More than enough money. More than enough happiness. And all within the framework of sustainability for yourself, your loved ones, and the planet. Imagine always being provided with an abundant supply of what you need when you need it. Imagine your body vibrant in vitality through all of this joy.

Create the Life You Want

The queen archetype within you is calling you to embody the healed Divine Feminine. Are you committed to your heroine's journey and creating the life you want, desire, require, and deserve? The Magic of Transformation in combination with sacred self-care to ground your dreams into prosperous reality will get you there but I am not going to lie. It does entail trust in the unfolding and faith to walk a journey that often is unpredictable. The ride can be a little wild, and it is most definitely an adventure. But once you fully commit to yourself and who you are becoming, you will bloom, blossom, prosper and thrive while experiencing profound healing, transformation, and Soul level empowerment. There currently is a global movement of wise women and medicine bearers healing the Divine Feminine and Sacred Masculine within themselves, so they can powerfully step into their purpose and Soul life. In sacred union within themselves, they show up as the queen they truly are to aid the people and the planet. I do want you to know that you can too.

Shine light on love. Shine light on the Divine. Shine a light on the darkness within you and trust yourself and the process. Shine light on your soul's inherited power to heal those spaces within you that are needing love and illumination for you to fully integrate them into wholeness.

REFLECTION AND INTEGRATION

1. Are you able to be present in your body, in the now moment? Or do you feel like you live outside of your body most of the time?
2. Do you regularly apply your strong nurturing skills for yourself? Or is your output more than your input?
3. Are you able to set effective limits and communicate healthy boundaries in life?
4. Do you know how to nourish, nurture and support yourself through life?
5. Do you understand balance at its core in terms of feminine and masculine energy?
6. How is your relationship with stress, proving your worth and your enoughness?
7. What is your relationship with pleasure like?

Chapter 9
A Family of Spiritual Seekers

You become what your deepest desire is.

As your desire is, so your intention.

As your intention is, so your will.

As your will, so is your deed.

As your deed, so is your destiny.

—Vedic Text

My parents, in their essence, were spiritual seekers in pursuit of finding their truth. They had wild dreams of creating their best life and finances while also doing good in the world. But in pursuit of their happiness and wildest dreams, they got very lost and entangled in old stories of karma.

They did not have the tools available to them to clear, cleanse, and clarify so that they could align their deepest Soul desire and heart's wish. They set plenty of intentions and made ample decisions to create more affluence, over and over again. But their actions came from an energetically noisy place. There was a lot of discord and incongruence in their energy they did not know about. How could they have known? They did not have tools to change this available to them.

I watched my parents struggle. They struggled in their relationship. They struggled with their finances. And they never realized their potential to fulfill their social promise to win big and do good in the world. It was witnessing their struggle that fanned the flames of my determination to find answers. I needed to understand this dissonance and incongruence. How could this be? How could they be thinking so positively and ambitiously and be in so much pain and manifesting so little results? How could this be? I just had to know!

Their striving for success and a better life for themselves, in turn, raised me and my brother in pursuit of the same. My brother and sister-in-law raise their two sons with the intention of conscious parenting and the purpose of helping them unfold their god-given potential as little Divine humans here on earth while also striving for their ideal lifestyle and ideal income. My husband and I live our lives in pursuit of our personal legends and happiness, living true to our heart and Soul, so we can fulfill our social promise. We, too, are devoted to creating our ideal lifestyle and income to support the life we desire. All of us have experienced huge gaps when it comes to the life we live and the life we aspire to. We understand the struggle and all the question marks that arise along the way.

I believe that there are vast numbers of spiritual seekers in our world. In pursuit of finding their truth and Soul Self so they can make this world a better place by just being in it. I believe these same spiritual seekers often struggle with finances or relationships. Some might even be experiencing health challenges on top of that. I believe you, the one reading this book, are part of this family of spiritual seekers aspiring to be your best self to be part of creating a better world for yourself and others. We are kindred spirits in this way.

You might be wondering what further qualities we share might look like. Thinking of my parents, my brother, my sister-in-law, my husband and myself, I would say that we love our independence. We like being able to respond to life in spontaneous and fun ways. We are curious, very insightful at times, enthusiastic, freedom-loving and innovative in how we approach the problems and challenges we face in life. We love having a purpose and approach life and people with an open heart and mind. We really dislike limitation and boredom in our lives. We are always game for explorations and expanding into the next level best version of ourselves. We all believe that life should be an adventure that is of service to the greater whole. Life should be fun! We, as spiritual seekers, have a natural Wanderlust, and we love creating life through conscious choices we make in alignment with our heart and Soul Self. We strive to learn how to express our Soul Selves here on earth, in this lifetime.

However, we also get very disillusioned by the current structure, systems, and affairs of the world and the lack of enlightenment, the lack of mind, body, spirit, heart connection. We realize that we too fall prey to social conditioning and the world of Ego—the rational mind that rationalizes absolutely everything. This type of reality and environment makes it quite challenging to stay true to our Soul Self paths at times. There is so much noise and distraction out there. Not all that shines is gold. Because of all of this, I believe it is time to show the world how creating a heart-centered, happy, wholesome, abundant Soul Self life is an absolute possibility. I dare say even a necessity for our survival. In this day and age, the world needs healers, teachers and guides if we are to awaken to our Divinity and our spiritual selves, as well as the Divine gifts we bring to this world, in service of it.

"When the personality comes fully to serve the energy of its Soul that is authentic empowerment." —Gary Zukov

When the mountain of our current structure, systems, and affairs seems insurmountable to climb, it gets hard to see the ripple effect that small little changes at a time can have on our global well-being. When bogged down by the heaviness of the daily grind, it is hard for us to see the good in ourselves and others. It is hard to acknowledge how each of us is just trying our best with what we have been given. When continuously discounting ourselves and others, feeling unappreciated and never quite enough, no matter what we do, life gets pretty miserable indeed.

When we add up the sum of all of these components: day after day, week after week, month after month, year after year, we can begin to sense that it will add up to no good. We cannot use rotten eggs and expect a delicious egg sandwich! We all know that. So why is it so hard to see that the quality of our thoughts, emotions, and actions will create our life experience and future?

Ask yourself:

- As a collective, are our quality of thoughts and actions based on fear or love?
- As a collective, are our quality of thoughts and actions based on Ego trips or Soul desires?
- Can you see that even spiritual seekers need to learn and see how creating a heart-centered, happy, wholesome, abundant Soul Self life is an absolute necessity for our survival as a species?

Self-ownership and self-responsibility are hard to accept for many because that would put them in the driver's seat of their life. It's the reason they choose not to do it. Their payoff is to blame, shame, or cuss out others, make them responsible.

- Can you see how that same mechanism also gives their power away to outside sources?
- Can you see how giving your power away like that creates an energy exchange and loop of victim and perpetrator?

- Can you see how we can only ever change ourselves and that it begins with taking ownership and embracing self-responsibility?

Owning that we have the power to create our own reality and experience will help us understand: if we created it, we could change it! Once we own that, we become the heroines of our lives, not the victims. Then the change, the healing, and the transformation we so desire as individuals, require as a collective, and simply deserve for being alive, can truly begin.

Creating Your Soul Self Expressed Abundant Life

“It begins with accepting total responsibility for every aspect of your life and refusing to blame anyone else. The degree to which you accept responsibility for everything in your life is precisely the degree of personal power you have to change or create anything in your life.” —Hal Elrod

Setting a Secure Foundation

It will take you building a secure foundation from which you can grow and expand into the best version of yourself and life. There are five components that I discovered in my search to find the answers and tools my parents did not have. I discovered the missing puzzle pieces to the bigger holistic picture in these components.

The Difference Between a Soul Inspired Desire and an Ego-Driven One

There is never just one side to a story. We all know that. My parents did the best they could with what they had. It wasn't their fault that they were missing tools and the puzzle pieces to make the bigger picture whole.

I personally was able to commit myself and my life to growth and transformation from an early age because of them. Even when it was the dysfunctional aspect of them. That does not matter. I made that heartfelt decision when I was 14. My intention to transcend, transmute, and transform has brought me here, writing this book. Sharing with you my discoveries. I have learned to identify wounds but can also find the Soul medicine that will heal them. I have become an alchemist turning heavy human experiences into spiritual gold. The kind of spiritual gold that will make you magnetic to your higher good so that you and your story tell a tale of victory as opposed to victimhood.

The very first foundational step to creating everything you desire, require and deserve as your Soul Self best version is taking ownership and accepting self-responsibility. This act is heart-based and soulful. It is not based in Ego nor rational mind. It is based on realizing that you never have the power over changing others, but you do hold the power to change yourself. It's a realization based on love and illumination. This illumination helps you understand that you cannot change what you cannot see. And you cannot heal what you cannot feel.

The Soul does not always invite you into growth and transformation with sparkles of inspiration, upliftment, and empowerment. More often than not, it is hitting rock bottom and the dark night of the Soul urging us to look at those things we have been avoiding. It's a time of seeing that which we couldn't see before, as well as a time of feeling those hard feelings to clear and cleanse ourselves from them. This then clarifies our sacred path here on earth as a Divine human being. Soul wants you to grow and expand your light here on earth, fulfilling your social promise.

Ego wants to keep you safe. Ego's job is to keep you safe at all costs. Ego cannot afford the status quo to change because how is it supposed to keep you safe in unchartered territory? Ego is part of your rational mind, the social conditioning and conformity training each one of us has undergone. Ego is also found in the oldest part of our brain and governs our survival instincts. Ego only has one job, and it is to keep you safe and alive! So it does what it knows and repeats what it is used to even if you don't like it because it keeps you safe and alive.

This is where consciousness, free will, and spiritual awareness come in. You have the power to override ego using your consciousness, free will, and the awareness of your Soul. However, it is a bit of a messy process that challenges you to leave your comfort zone. Many people don't change and choose to stay stuck because the devil you know is better than the one you don't.

The Remaining Puzzle Pieces

Setting an intention is making a decision

Setting the intention to want to discover your Soul Self to create your best life is a decision you make. Decisions, just like thoughts, live in the fourth-dimensional aspect of you while your Soul Self is the fifth-dimensional aspect of you.

Following through with a decision is a choice

Only choices truly affect your life and your positive or negative karma. Choices are decisions you made followed up with action. The action you take makes it a choice you made. Just thinking about stuff does absolutely nothing.

Choices create your life

It is important for you to understand the process of anchoring Soul Self here on earth and how choices you make are key to that anchoring. Choices you make express your Divinity, or they can take you away from your Divinity. So choices you make can either be Soul aligned or Soul Self misaligned. Your choices will create your life experience.

Conscious choice creates your heart-centered life

Conscious choices, choices made with an awareness of your Soul, hold the power and potential of creating your little piece of heaven here on earth. Imagine as many people as possible awakening to this power and potential, creating their space of heavenly, Divine love, power, truth. This would truly change our world, wouldn't it? Become the change you wish to see in the world, right?

Congruence in spirit, mind, heart and body manifests the alchemy: the Magic of Transformation

- Soul is the fifth-dimensional aspect of you, a realm of Spirit.
- Making a decision based on a soul-inspired idea pulls Spirit into the 4th dimension, your mental realm.
- Your heart and emotions are the gateways between the 4th & 3rd dimension, your emotional realm.
- Running a clean, clear current of emotions through your heart will give you the strength and courage to take action on your Soul-inspired idea, making it a choice in the 3rd dimension. The physicality of this world.
- Soul-aligned choice after choice creates your desired outcome in our 3rd-dimensional physical world while you are living, breathing, expressing, and embodying your divinity.

REFLECTION AND INTEGRATION

1. Do you identify with a family of spiritual seekers, or are you the only one in your family seeking?
2. What are you looking to create and experience in your life?
3. How do you discern between soul-inspired ideas and ego-driven ones?
4. How do you experience your Divinity and creating heaven on earth?

Chapter 10
A Mother's Love and a Daughter's Healing

Dad passed in April of 2014, at age 84, and Mum passed in October of 2020, at age 80. As I was writing this book and nearing completion, we got the sudden news that mum fell ill and would not recover. We were urged to come to see her one last time as the doctor expressed this to be mum's explicit wish. Four members of the family were able to travel to Germany from the US, South Africa and Great Britain during Covid times and the pandemic. It truly felt magical and like a miracle, to be honest.

The breakdown of her physical body arrived suddenly, and her death came fast. It was unexpected for all of her family members and lifelong friends. Dad's passing involved a lot of healing around the Father Wound and us coming to terms with him not providing for his family in the way he could have. It was coming to terms with the parts in us that were grieving that he did not do what we wished he would have done. Mum's passing and transition was quite different. It involved graduating from healing the Mother Wound, co-dependency and enmeshment as a mother/daughter team. This opened up a magical portal of grace, ease and profound healing and transformation for both of us. The grieving process for me involved coming to terms with my parents having a less than perfect marriage and wishing that mum had left my dad to find her own empowered and liberated path.

Our mother/daughter relationship was not an easy one as it often goes for mothers and daughters that are too much alike. Daughters are not willing to step into their mother's footsteps because they'd rather trail-blaze their own path. I do realize that I am part of a new generation of women that had opportunities open up to them that the generations before them did not have. However, even as trailblazers, we often still carry the wounds of the feminine lineage in our DNA.

During mum's transition, I was gifted with many insights and illuminations about her as a woman and mother. I could see clearly how truly amazing she was. She, too, was a fierce Warrior Goddess. Working on her empowerment with what she had available. I could honor that I, as her daughter of a different generation, was given more tools and opportunities of empowerment in my lifetime.

The biggest gift mum gave me as she transitioned was the gift of unconditional and undying Love. Mum showed me how she chose love over fear, even when I was a difficult, stubborn, and headstrong daughter trailblazing her own path in life. She showed me how her unconditional love for me, as well as her willingness to show up for personal growth, was able to heal the rift between us. In her death and transition, she showed me how it mended the disconnect to feminine power in our lineage.

Through the Akashic Records, I was able to find out that our healing contract for this lifetime was fulfilled. Realizing that the celebration and graduation energy I was so palpably sensing as she passed was real because we both had just gone through a spiritual graduation of sorts. We were celebrating how we healed our relationship as mother and daughter, how we came into our feminine power as women, and how much love we felt for each other and found living in our hearts. It was easy to let go of old resentments in an instant and realize that all that matters, in the end, is how much love capacity our heart can expand into in one lifetime. We were celebrating how our mother/daughter healing path contributed to the healing of our whole divine feminine lineage.

With mum's passing, I was able to witness how the energy work we did through Soul Realignment and clearing karma in the Akashic Records can course correct and rectify a life path. This type of spiritual growth and personal development work reconnects us to our Divinity as we are incarnate as humans walking the earth. It can transmute and transform long-held pain so that it does not need to be repeated over and over again. It transforms the often heavy leaden human experience into the lightness of realized spiritual gold and potential. With the Magic of Transformation taking place, we create a new space. Space where love can grow, nourishment takes root, nurturing and support are present. Space where we receive our life force directly from Soul Self and light-filled essence. Co-dependency and enmeshment are no longer required because we learn how to powerfully stand on our own. Sourcing from our own root system and Divinity. With our life force energy cleared and intact, we now have all the energy available to us to create all we require, desire, and deserve as women to lead our fully expressed Soul life.

Our spiritual graduation involved recognizing and letting go of long held onto patterns. You see, what mum mostly taught me wasn't through the things she was saying but rather through the things she was showing me, modeling for me.

Mum was a great healer with untapped potential and spiritual gifts. She was an amazing person, but she didn't believe she was worthy. So yes, when I grew up, I figured that I wanted to do better than that in life. She did teach me to have integrity, live life with joy, do what I love, and marry whomever I want but to make sure that we communicate properly. She taught me that communication is everything. I don't blame her for not feeling worthy of having money. I understand that she was not able to teach me about being financially empowered as a woman because this topic was never talked about in her family of origin. I get that this "not talking about having money as a woman" somehow translated for her to not feel deserving of having it for herself—so she settled.

Healing Ancestral Lines of the Divine Feminine

For the last decade, mum and I talked about how to foster:

- Connection to Self
- Connection to Body Wisdom
- Connection to Heart's Wishes & Desires
- Heart to Heart Connection with Others
- Connection to Higher Self
- Connection to Spirit Dream Team & Guides
- Connection to Source
- Connection to Soul's Purpose & Soul's Evolution

It was those conversations and showing up for what needed to change that healed the Mother Wound, the co-dependency and enmeshment, even the Father Wound. It's a feminine approach, not a masculine one. The feminine is dark like the womb that births the sacred. It takes getting comfortable with the dark to heal it and integrate it. Mum and I were kindred spirits and still are. Even beyond the veil, we continue to have 'conversations' about this. The type of conversations that spiritual seekers in pursuit of their truth, power, love, and Soul Self love to have.

Mum was in pursuit of her truth, power and love until the day she died. Her Ego mind wrongly telling her that her life was full of failure and mishaps, missed opportunities and misplaced heart's wishes. During the transition, this lie was cleared as we could both feel, sense and hear our Souls speaking to each other through the heart. The last decade had us prepared for this. This last decade we connected in ways that were driven by the heart and Soul and love.

I could sense and feel how mum could see her life clearly now, beyond the veil of illusions that often obstructs our Soul's clarity. There was such spaciousness, grand love, and so much peace and joy around her and in this situation that it was hard for me to feel sad. I felt so happy for her, my mum. For us and all the healing, we activated as a mother/daughter team. All I could do was celebrate her and her life at this time of her transition. The grieving part and letting go of her physical presence were not at the forefront for me as she was transitioning. I could feel her happy and peaceful, reflecting on her life. Realizing that she did us good as a mum. She really did. It wasn't perfect. It wasn't always easy, but it was good and wholesome and, most importantly, filled with so much love. Love does conquer all in the end. It really does.

"Releasing doership means that rather than striving and pushing harder, you actually learn to get out of the way." —Tosha Silver

With the energy of graduation in the air, I let go of the physical aspect of Mum Jamiela while honoring her essence and true nature. Love. Mum always spoke of herself as a late bloomer, but the thing that became very clear during her transition was how her Soul bloomed and grew in this lifetime. And most of all, how a mother's love, however imperfectly it shows up, can catalyze and support a daughter's healing if she's willing to receive it. I was receiving it fully, and with it, we were able to clear the pain of a whole line of women before us as she transitioned.

I can now see that it is my Soul-inspired desire to show women how Soul Realignment energy work can clear, clarify, transmute and transform long-held pain in 2021 and beyond.

Showing women how this clearing, clarifying and healing opens them up to receive more nourishment, Divine guidance, and continued support from their Soul Self and light-filled essence so that they can create all they require, desire, and deserve.

REFLECTION AND INTEGRATION

1. What is your relationship with your mother like?
2. What is your relationship with your father like?
3. Have you heard of the Mother Wound?
4. Have you heard of the Father Wound?
5. Have you heard of co-dependency and enmeshment family patterns?
6. What is your relationship with co-dependence and enmeshment?
7. How do you feel about all of this? What do you need? And do you need support?

Chapter 11
The Magic of Transformation

It's a Fire Path

Soul Realignment activates the fire of potential, our confidence and trust in ourselves in the form of empowerment and Divine inspiration. When we harness and direct our inner abilities to transform situations, we find ourselves in seats of power and sustenance. It takes broadening our scope of thinking and being in the world, as well as taking action. Through taking aligned action, you learn to be dynamic, claim your personal power, allow your light to shine brightly and feel passionate about life.

Soul Realignment activates the inner fire. Fire is the element that invites you into the dynamic and transformative aspects of yourself. It encompasses your sense of self, relationship to others, and relationships to your ancestors and lineage. It contains the self and all of its many, and sometimes very messy, aspects: the Ego, self-perception, and self-worth. Its lesson calls us to synchronize and harmonize our inner selves with the world's outer self.

The Magic of Transformation activates your outer fire and is your initiation to take action in your life, in service of your highest and best self. This action entails learning how to tend your fire effectively and safely. If you are adequately managing your fire to activate the magic of your transformation, you feel empowered to change anything in your life.

Be it:

- family dynamics and relationships
- career, vocation and profession
- your livelihood and the way you create your income
- your health, your wealth, and your relationships with the world at large

If, however, there is a lot of energetic noise in your system, it is hard to align your actions and firepower to achieving your desired outcome. Misaligned energy then creates misalignment in your results by the law of attraction. Noisy energy in your system also gets you overanalyzing and overthinking instead of moving yourself forward effectively and gracefully while anchored in simplicity.

Soul Realignment and the Magic of Transformation in combination is a fire path that invites you to look at your internal thermostat to see how you can cultivate a fully expressed life anchored in your Divinity, as well as a healthy fire element as your foundation. The healthy fire element will ask you to create a healthy relationship with the other elements in your life too.

Earth and water represent the feminine aspects in you. Fire and air representing the masculine aspects in you. In all-encompassing health and wealth, these elements come together into the unified field of creation and Spirit. In this unified field of creation, you are rooted to rise and sourcing the full capacity of your power, love and truth. This power, this love, and this truth then create your Magic and embodied Soul Self here on earth.

What does a healthy fire element look like?

What is the positive polarity of the fire element expressed?

You feel comfortable in altered states of awareness, such as meditation. Stopping, slowing down, breathing, and listening.

You feel dynamic, joyous and energetic.

You take action! Feeling juiced with your inner firepower.

Your aligned action helps you grow.

You are illuminated with insights, and your Divine guidance is lighting your path.

Letting go is easy for you.

Your life force energy pulsates through your body, and you know how to direct it in a safe and efficient way.

You move!

You are passionate about life!

You enjoy the power of action!

You are expressing your Radiant Self to the world!

You enjoy sensuality and sexuality!

You love money!

You enjoy that spark of transformation!

You cherish the warmth of your inner fire, giving you the resilience to make all your dreams come true!

What does the negative polarity look like? How does an unhealthy fire element express?

It's hard for you to sit still. Quieting your mind to meditate is near impossible, and quite frankly, you feel it's a waste of your precious time. You have things to do and places to be.

You feel strained, drained, and running on empty.

Deep down, you know that you are burning your candle at both ends.

You know that this isn't healthy or sustainable, but you don't know how to be any other way.

You have an excessively busy schedule. You are very busy but not effective in your results.

You feel confused and unclear as to why all your actions and busyness are not bringing you the results you want.

You have an insatiable drive to move forward, achieve and accomplish.

You use caffeine, sugar, and simple carbs to keep you energized, stoked, and receiving quick bursts of energy.

Or you barely eat all day to then really indulge in large portions of healthy food and healthy snacking at night.

Your body is suffering from indigestion, burping, stomach upsets, intolerances to food, allergies, unhealthy accumulation of belly fat.

It's hard for you to let go.

You don't exercise. You work.

You have a love and hate relationship with money.

You crave sex and intimacy but cannot relax enough to open yourself up to receive that pleasure.

Balance is hard for you. It's either all the way turned on or all the way turned off.

REFLECTION AND INTEGRATION

1. Ask Earth, what messages she has for you to more fully embody wholeness?
2. Ask Water, how you are being called to develop a greater sense of emotional maturity?
3. Ask Air, is it time to activate daily meditation and prayer?
4. Ask Fire, how can you assist me in living my life energized and enlivened without burning myself out?
5. Ask Spirit, how are you currently teaching me through the *As Within/So Without* mysteries?

Next Steps

Congratulations! You have almost finished reading this short, helpful book on how to ignite your Soul's desires and manifesting them by applying the Magic of Transformation. I trust that by now, your heart is open and lit. Your mind has grown to recognize how your true nature is showing up in your life. It is my intention to support your decision to create a fully Soul Self expressed life.

I wrote this book to be a starting point for our relationship, and as I see it, you have three opportunities in front of you right now.

1. You can close this book and do nothing with the story and reflective questions I shared. If you have gotten this far, I sure hope this is not an option for you.
2. You can start listening to your heart and Soul on your own by leveraging the reflective journaling questions and begin the journey of your Soul's quest.
3. You can make the wise decision to schedule a Soul Realignment Blueprint Session to discuss a reading, healing and Akashic clearing session with me. There are no obligations, and booking this free connection call is non-binding. Scheduling is really easy, and really, ask yourself: what do I have to lose? Maybe we are meant to work together. Maybe not. But we will not know until we actually connect to have this conversation. Visit

Happywholesomelife.as.me to easily schedule this complimentary connection call.

I Know Your Soul Desires Are Whispering

I know Soul desires are whispering in your heart and encouraging you to grow and expand into your Divinity so you can become Soul Self walking the earth. Bridging the gap between heaven and earth. But I also know that the voice of your Ego and rational mind can potentially scream far louder than your heart or Soul. At this point, I want you to realize that you can choose to be the conscious creator of your life experience. You can change what you do not like. You don't have to know the how. Sometimes all it takes is the courage to listen to your heart and Soul by taking that first step. The choice is yours, and regardless of which path you take, I trust that I have inspired you to start listening to your own magic—The Magic of Transformation. The magic your heart and Soul are calling you to.

Remember what Marrianne Williamson said and Nelson Mandela shared with the world:

"Our deepest fear is not that we are inadequate. Our deepest fear is that we are powerful beyond measure. It is our light, not our darkness that most frightens us. We ask ourselves, Who am I to be brilliant, gorgeous, talented, fabulous? Actually, who are you *not* to be?

You are a child of God. Your playing small does not serve the world. There is nothing enlightened about shrinking so that other people won't feel insecure around you. We are all meant to shine, as children do. We were born to make manifest the glory of God that is within us. It's not just in some of us; it's in everyone. And as we let our own light shine, we unconsciously give other people permission to do the same. As we are liberated from our own fear, our presence automatically liberates others."

If I can be of service to you, please let me know and best wishes as you move forward.

From my heart to yours,

Nadia S. Krauss

Appendix

Helpful Resources

- The Seat of the Soul by Gary Zukov
- Unlock Your Intuition by Andrrea Hess
- My video series: How the Unhealed Mother Wound Affects You During Peri-Menopause

You can sign up for the webinar here:

https://www.happywholesomelife.com/sign-up/

Frequently Asked Questions

How do I know if Soul Realignment is for me?

Most of my clients come to work with me because they know, like and trust me and out of a deep desire to understand the nature of their Soul so they can express themselves at the level of Soul, furthering their own spiritual revolution and conscious creation in their lifetime. Some are already active in the healing arts but are craving an even deeper level.

What can I expect when booking the FREE Soul Realignment Blueprint Session?

In our session together, we will be able to determine on a personal level if we are a fit in regards to working together. You know, that know, like and trust factor that is so important for both parties involved. It also gives me a chance to determine if your Soul is saying yes to this work, not just your personality. I am able to confirm this by checking in the Akashic Records prior to the session. You are also able to ask any questions you might have about the process of a Soul Realignment reading, healing, and clearing.

What happens after the assessment?

If it is a yes, we set up an appointment and payment details. If it is a no, you can be assured that I do not engage in any hard selling, manipulative, aggressive sales tactics. I will never make you feel bad for your clarity. I might invite you to any of my free gifts, offers, and community to stay in touch if I see there is a need for it.

About Nadia Shana Krauss

When I wake up in the morning, the very first inspiring thought and empowering emotion found inside of me, is, 'What will I choose to create today?'

After that, a joyous KNOWING: 'Something great is going to happen today! I can feel it.'

I believe in the power of self ~ love ~ leadership, and making choices that support a happy, wholesome, abundant and prosperous life.

My heart literally glows when I see women empowering themselves through their Sacred Self-care practice ~ spiritually, mentally, emotionally, physically.

My heart breaks a little when I see women believing that they don't have choices they can make and that they need to continue to hustle, to stress, to 'chase the madness' so they can 'prove their enough-ness' to the world.

I know that this false belief can be transformed by diving deep into personal growth and development of Self through Soul Realignment & feminine empowerment work.

My readers, clients, and members of my online platforms are my soul tribe and kindred spirit sisters.

More than anything else, I care about helping them to be the heroine of their own life, by supporting them in their choices. Choices create your life experience!

I cheer them on as they powerfully manifest their dreams while fully anchored in their Radiance so that they can experience all they require, desire, and deserve!

In my world, love, laughter, joy, and abundance are absolute necessities. And DANCING, celebrating, and giving thanks, is always a fabulous idea. 'Perfect' is overrated, and 'faking' is a definite NO. Fantasizing about dancing on stage with Beto Perez and the Zumba Crew is totally reasonable. Striving for a wholesome, heart-centered Soul life is a must.

At the end of the day, all that really matters is how much light, love, joy, power, love, and truth I lived, embodied, spread and shared. I walk my own talk and take my own medicine.

When I die, I want to be remembered as a woman who empowered, uplifted, and inspired others to BE the change they wish to see in this world. I wish to be remembered as the powerful & joyous force that I AM. I want to be remembered as one that ignited that same force in others.

My websites and online scheduler

www.nadiakrauss.com

www.selfloveleadership.com

www.happywholesomelife.as.me

A small favor

Thank you for reading *The Magic of Transformation.* I trust that reading this book has served you well. Would you mind taking a minute or two and leaving an honest review for this book on Amazon? Reviews are the best way to help others purchase this book, and I check all my reviews looking for helpful feedback.

If you have any questions or if you would just like to tell me about your “A-ha’s,” insights, and breakthroughs while reading this book, write an email to

Nadia@happywholesomelife.com. I’d love to hear from you!

www.ingramcontent.com/pod-product-compliance
Lightning Source LLC
LaVergne TN
LVHW010105110826
845155LV00028B/491
* 9 7 8 1 9 5 1 1 3 1 1 8 0 *